INNER LANDSCAPE

POEMS

by

MAY SARTON

Martino Publishing
Mansfield Centre, CT
2016

Martino Publishing
P.O. Box 373,
Mansfield Centre, CT 06250 USA

ISBN 978-1-68422-008-3

© *2016 Martino Publishing*

Cover Design Tiziana Matarazzo

Printed in the United States of America On 100% Acid-Free Paper

INNER LANDSCAPE

POEMS

by

MAY SARTON

THE CRESSET PRESS
LONDON

FOR

JULIAN AND JULIETTE HUXLEY

Grateful acknowledgment is made for the use of poems printed in POETRY: A MAGAZINE OF VERSE, TIME AND TIDE, THE LONDON MERCURY, HARPER'S BAZAAR, THE SATURDAY REVIEW OF LITERATURE.

CONTENTS

ENCOUNTER IN APRIL (1929-1933)

I

FROM THIS NETTLE
(1936-1938)

Ah! Rien au monde n'est plus confus, n'est moins tranquille,
O souvenir! que ton pauvre visage humain!—

JEAN DOMINIQUE

PRAYER BEFORE WORK

★

Great one, austere,
By whose intent the distant star
Holds its course clear,
Now make this spirit soar—
Give it that ease.

Out of the absolute,
Abstracted grief, comfortless, mute,
Sound the clear note,
Pure, piercing as the flute:
Give it precision.

Austere, great one,
By whose grace the inalterable song
May still be wrested from
The corrupt lung:
Give it strict form.

3

INVOCATION

*

Be marble, O ice out of fire!
The small Egyptian head
The sculptor's warm desire
Matched to the stone and perfected.

Be music, O precision of a dream!
Fashion of algebraic phrase and note
This diffused passion to a single theme,
O piercing as the flute, O sweet cold throat!

Be the abstraction, be the essence,
Inhuman, without hunger,
Receive, reflect, accept the freighted sense,
Endure its weight no longer.

Be marble, music: freeze and entrance
The blood until its measure move
As ponderable as stone beneath your glance—
But be my love!

ARCHITECTURAL IMAGE

★

Whatever finds its place now in this edifice
Must be a buttress to the spire's strict arrow,
No arbitrary grace, no facile artifice
Beyond its compass, absolute and narrow,

Structure imponderable in its ascension,
It is the central nerve, the living spine,
Within it there exists a soaring tension,—
Flight, but deriving from the sternest line.

Whatever arches mould to gentle curve,
Whatever flowers are carved into its face,
Are thrown, are carved to decorate and serve
That motion of a finger into space.

All that is builded here is built to bind
The gentle arch, the stone flower of desire
Into the sterner vision of the mind:
The structure of this passion is a spire.

5

LANDSCAPE

*

It is a different landscape to the one you know,
No wind, no cloud's distraction for the eye,
Only this white earth changed as if by snow,
Brilliant reflected purity of endless sky.

Life is maintained here at expenditure of spirit.
The weak are dazzled, go blind under the powerful light,
The faint heart bleeds in ether and cannot endure it,
The mind may lose its measure in a day without night.

But, O my love, look at the infinite spaces,
Walk where our feet together make no sound, and slow,
With that unearthly light that falls across men's faces
When words freeze on the mouth, lie down in the snow.

Here is the fire that burns through ice warmly and still,
Here the mind frozen up can never intercede:
Feel how the stubborn heart captures your will,
Burns in the breast so hotly that it cannot bleed.

Here in this strange snow-landscape, brightanddesolate,
Find at the end the simplest, the most lucid peace,
Passion that takes a perfect form and stays inviolate,
Spirit accompanied in the wilderness: I give you these.

RECORD

★

Let us record this autumn, set it apart forever
Not as a season only but accompaniment
To a pervading human mood and its endeavor
In you not to partake of what is imminent.

The heart suffers no torrent like this for a breath,
Nor spends itself to celebrate a season,
It is no leaf to burn then freeze to death:
These words are written with impassioned reason.

And this is autumn. Leaves fall one by one.
This morning I went out after the frost to watch them
Break off, green still, in the cold sun,
As if a careful hand must quietly detach them.

But if this tree stands now with leaves just turning,
If each must be despoiled and the cold hand break it:
Let it be recorded that love stood beside you burning,
Let it be remembered forever that you did not partake it.

LAMENT

★

Love is the least thing offering itself alone.
What for a gift is this crying in the bone?
Mute torrent in the eye that fears to weep,
The childish seeking mouth, the final sleep?
If it were snow it would fall soft as wool,
Wrapping the senses with a silken spool.
If it were music it would charm, unbind
With waterfalls of sound the aching mind.
If it were sleep it would shut the eye fast,
O too aware, too clear, shut the moth-wing at last!
It would say to you, 'Here is passion deeper than death,'—
This love so lightly freighted with a human breath.

UNDERSTATEMENT

*

This wind, corruption in the city,
(Spirit pent up in an enclosure),
That steals, seductive, without pity,
The heart's composure.

Think of it gusting over a field today,
Setting the cows to lowing with surprise,
Spreading the sweet smell of manure and hay,
Bringing tears to the eyes.

Oh, there are places where this evil wind
Would work a blessed charm,
Where a wild thing like this warm wind
Would do no harm.

GRANTED THIS WORLD

*

Granted this world is an imagined one,
Existing in the mind, only the mind,
And it will vanish in the actual sun,
Having no power to turn the clear eye blind.

A cool glass country where the heavy green
Fruit hangs untouchable, transparent,
Flowers not to be touched but only seen:
Nothing is real yet everything apparent.

Here we have come believing the desire
To break a flower is a dream of the hand
To which it cannot in reality aspire—
Where petals are of glass, you understand.

And yet we move, are without question moving,
Out of this room, this chair, this certain hour
To that imagined country, the fruit-loving,
Where the hand shatters the glass flower,

The moment when the unbeliever sees
The warm blood trickle on the actual wrist,
Where the imagined orchard of glass trees
Yields flower and fruit into the wounded fist.

Though he must wake to find it as before,
Himself still sitting in that room, that chair
No shattered crystal fruit upon the floor,
No treasure in his hand that was not there.

Granted this world is an imagined place
(Real and unreal are easily divisible)
But what then of the anguish on his face?
The wound is there although invisible.

The fruit is picked, broken the glassy rind,
The flower on the floor and shattered,
Though it existed only in the mind,
This orchard—though it never mattered.

II

SONNETS

Is this heart, emperor, setting at your feet
A city full of captives and their treasure,
Or sleight of hand, a juggler in the street
With feathered toys designed to give you pleasure?
If the imperial heart, the hand devout
Had played for your applause, had hoped to please
We should have fumbled, fallen, been found out,
Having no tricks we can perform with ease,
No art of begging who were born to give:
These words are ruled with pure ferocity,
Mastered like alien tribes and brought in captive
After a bloody war waged with no pity:
They are presented in a royal fashion—
No pleasure-city, but that empire, passion!

2

Not for my sake who have desired it so
But that this confined love suits you so poorly,
This cold, this barren desert that you show,
Where, innocent, the source still wells up surely,
Where, you admit, quick essence of the fountain
Cruelly buried by you, still is there,
And through the rock comes, through the weight of
        mountain,
Surrounds you like a perfume in the air:
The twig of the diviner feels the shock
Of living waters and is struck with wonder,
Hunting the voices hidden in the rock,
Feeling the power of the torrent thunder
That pulls him down to lean against the earth
As if his heart must help the difficult birth.

I had not dreamed this touch would turn to stone,
Foreseeing change but not this icy will,
This frozen acid eating to the bone,
Your hand withdrawn professing me no ill—
Foreseeing some end soon, true end or sterile,
But not this subtle and destructive blight;
A valiant marble head it was, in peril,
But all flushed through with a warm glowing light,
Informing gesture with its implication,
Informing silence to be rich and strange,
Informing mind with delicate sensation:—
You who now work a bitter fruitless change,
Stop up with tenderness the open vein
Where the cold marble bears no living stain.

4

But touch is means and signifies no more
At last in this seduction of the spirit
Than in a verse, caress of metaphor,
And there are other means love can inherit.
O sweeter, subtler than the flush of wine
This fever in the mind shall stain your cheek,
Shall set that very poison in the spine.
Though you are silent, though you will not speak
This room is charged now with an atmosphere—
You must be caught. You cannot break the spell.
Enchantment of a curious kind is here;
We are seduced, my love, you know it well—
Though with this heavy head against your breast
The knocking heart must still deny it rest.

5

Oh child look down, look down, your open eyes
Ravish the spirit without charity,
More innocent than is your heart, less wise,
Too pure, too clear, deceptive clarity:
O now look down and let me re-discover
The face you will, the mouth so well-defended
Against assault by this or any lover,
And then beneath the wiser lid suspended
Give me your silence, perfectly composed,
Let me explore the shape of the will there
Like music in a marble head enclosed—
So that this living hand upon your hair
May seem to listen in suspense above it,
Not suffer love, but be reminded of it.

6

For you who should have stood beside me here
Let me now praise this blessed piece of earth,
These pastures, cedar trees, this juniper,
This house with windows full of flowers, this hearth,—
See, I shall bring you pleasures one by one,
The patch of moss where you can lie full length,
The soft blond fields of grass in the pale sun,
The oak that you must hug to feel its strength;
See, I shall bring you everything we found—
The bright bunched berry of the pulpit-jack,
The creeping pine that wreathes the leafy ground,
All that the summer spent and now gives back:
Take from my hand this seed of the wild rose
And feel how in your hand the autumn glows.

7

Alone I may be, but still twice aware:
This imposed silence holds a vaster sound
Than cymbals or the trumpets' icy blare,
To one who lies with heart upon the ground
And looks up at the blazing winter heaven.
There planets, seeming motionless for years,
Still swim a fiery pattern, two and seven,
Making a music in the silent spheres—
Music more piercing than the mortal sense
Unless made twice aware can comprehend:
Through you, although alone, still twice intense
And stubborn in this night without an end
The soundless heart your heart could stoop to bless
Hears thundering music in the emptiness.

8

Because this strange adventure is so grave
As well as fraught with singular delight
It grows with grandeur like a mounting wave,
Born in the center of the ocean's might,
Bearing a distant past upon its wake
And these imagined worlds, these inner seas
Whose peaceful depths it draws up to partake,
Gathers its slow strength with a great wave's ease,
Comes on with an unerring silent motion,
Through locking waters to its steadfast home:
It rides the tempest of the troubled ocean,
Moves to the shore where it must shock in foam,
Where love implacable as stone must serve
To break the tension of the mounting curve.

9

Deny the passion that is bound in you,
Locked up in every secret part and caught,
Now like a quicksilver to course you through,
A lightning in the blood swifter than thought;
Now planted like a root whose thrust must pierce
The very house of which it is a guest,
Breaking those walls though they are strong and fierce,
Till you must bear it living in your breast,
Till you must suffer it to touch your marrow,
Plant there the tree no wind will ever shake,
The root of love like an embedded arrow,
Till in the unkissed palm the nerves' long ache
Cries out at last their hunger and their thirst,
Must come to bless this mouth that they have cursed!

There is no strength of words, none hard and pure,
None incorruptible as gold to clasp,
To bear this added weight and still endure,
To hold this treasure in their fragile grasp—
Fit to be freighted with the mind alone
They must bear now the hard head on the breast,
The living fertile womb cased in the bone,
Sweet flesh of which the spirit is a guest;
They must bear up two lovers, close-entwined,
Bear the full charge of mortal sweet embrace,
Hold the whole earth these hands have here defined,
Discovered, worshipped in a human face:
Words have no strength for this, the heart must take
In silence on itself although it break.

Defeat, here where we need not move nor speak,
Where no deed you or I can now perform
Will bring the heart down from the icy peak
Where it has climbed, serene, safe from all harm?
Defeat, where heart defines its impotence,
Survives the separation from desire,
Masters the pitiful tears, the angry sense
And stands superior to its own fire?
Turn back now if you must the rising flood,
The peace we should have shared, set it aside;
Suffer the solitary anguish of the blood.
This you may do but not deny the pride
That will, in triumph, decorate the bone
While the heart climbs, serene, to stand alone.

Yet pluck out from this nettle a brave flower,
Though you are all hemmed in with stinging weed,
A place sown with distress, and in this hour
Where courage fails you and your fingers bleed—
Did you set out to win a peaceful land,
An easier dream, was this your enterprise,
Who now cry out against your stinging hand?
This prickly country is that paradise.
Here in this place that seems so desolate,
Here at this time and set about with danger,
Still is your heaven here who hesitate
As if your former pride were now a stranger—
O heart, faint heart, have you no braver mettle,
To pluck the flower from the armèd nettle?

III

SUMMARY

SUMMARY

*

In the end it is the dark for which all lovers pine.
They cannot bear the light on their transparent faces,
The light on nerves exposed like a design.
They have a great need of sleep in foreign places,
Of another country than the heart and another speech.
In the end it is escape of which all lovers dream
As men in prison dream of a stretch of beach.
When they toss wide-eyed in their beds they may seem
To think of the cruel mouth and the hard breast
But it is simply murder that their hearts conceive,
Grown savage with the need of dark and rest.
They are ever innocent. They are found to believe
That love endures and their pain is infinite
Who have not learned that each single touch they give,
Every kiss, every word they speak holds death in it:
They are committing murder who merely live.

CONVERSATION ON THE TELEPHONE

*

Instant communication.
This is the modern torture:
the body jerked
from its relaxed position,
precipitated without will
into a situation
it can perceive
with one sense only.
The tension of the ear,
open and innocent
toward whatever voice leaps out,
inviting to a cocktail,
or a sale of Chelsea—
renouncing love.
It will drop like a hawk,
catching the mouse of anguish
as it tries to run.
It will suddenly stop,
no cry, no clamor bring it back,
no way of knowing where
in what room, in what city
the disembodied creature
has departed,
laughing or weeping?

This is the slicing off of ears
and cutting tongues,
the cruel modern severance
of one part from another,
as it clutches a dead instrument
and is asked,
'What number?'

ADDRESS TO THE HEART

★

You cannot go back now to that innocence—
the pure pain that enters like a sword
making the bright blood flow
and the slow perfect healing, leaving you whole.
This is a deeper illness,
a poison that has entered every tissue:
Cut off your hand, you will not find it there.
This must be met and conquered in each separate atom,
must be lived out like a slow fever.
No part is mortally afflicted.
Each part will have its convalescence surely,
and yet you will arise from this infection
changed,
as one returns from death.

TRANSITION

★

Here we are living in complete suspense,
There is a layer of time on earth, a snow;
Beneath the planted foot there is a silence,
The step falls soundlessly without an echo.

This world is negative, without precision,
We wander in it but cannot make a path,
We move across it in perpetual transition,
Perpetual journeying without an aftermath.

The light is half-light. If we fall asleep
It is to dream of an identical white landscape
Where we are never lost and never weep,
But where there is no rest and no escape.

This world is silence, an interminable season,
Suspense, a curious distorted place,
So that the young are ageless but will wizen,
The shape of lost direction on their face.

Interminable as snow time falls in silence,
Covering the little holes our feet have made,
We who are wanderers in complete suspense—
Who were the living and still are not the dead.

TRANSLATION

★

Silence the sound of bells in the high tower!
Curb this defeat which touches every sense,
Give the clear mind which it cannot disturb
Power for deafness in a ringing silence.

Translated inward out of the loud clamor,
Perish, attack upon the outward ear,
But in the inner auricle still flourish,
Hammer the sound within. Bells, be translated!

Till passion can come back again to living,
Deep out of touch with physical defeat,
Deep out of silence, action out of sleep,
Giving a secret power to the will.

THE VANQUISHED

*

Do not think for an instant that I will bear your pity
Across my mouth like a soft January rain—
Though you have plundered the walls and sacked the city
All this you shall see builded up, made stalwart again.
Do not think for a moment that I who have born
Love like a banner always, though now so tattered,
Would welcome pity to mend where it is torn.
The walls of this city are down. The walls are shattered.
But something is streaming still from the rampart
Vermilion against the sky. It is a proud pennant.
In its name this city was vanquished and torn apart,
In its name will be builded again, the flag dominant:
This is a brilliance that does not need your pity
For love builds out of defeat a deathless city.

MEMORY OF SWANS

★

The memory of swans comes back to you in sleep;
The landscape is a currentless still stream
Where reeds and rushes stand fast-rooted, deep.
And there the marvelous swan, more white than cream,
More warm than snow, moves as if silence loved him,
Where the dark supple waters ripple and enlace
The soft curve of the breast but have not moved him,
Where fluid passion yields to that cold grace.

So swans proceed, a miracle of pomp across your sleep,
The birds of silence, perfect form and balanced motion:
How will you fashion love, how will you wake and keep
The pride, the purity of a great image freed of its emotion?

AFTER SILENCE

*

Permit the eye so long lost in the inward night
Now to rejoice upon the outward forms of light;
Permit the mind return from those dark secret mazes
To rest a moment in these simple praises;
Permit the spirit homecoming from civil war
To poise itself on silence like a quiet star
That for this moment there may be no other will
Than to be silent, than to be absolutely still—
And then permit this human love to bless
Your further journey into solitariness.

CANTICLES

Behind what little mirror lies the country of your voice?
What rivers the heart has seen but never the open eyes?
What was your instrument, what rainy flute your choice,
What lucid language, lighter than our human cries
Did you once speak to call this voice your own?
No bird could hold such grief in its slight throat,
No human anguish sing like light enmeshed in rain,
Is it a spirit then, composed of immaterial note—
And if you are that spirit in a mirror's face
How can one reach you, unreflected, in a human place?

2

As music in a still house out of silence springs,
Causing the secret waters of the mind to flow,
As like a crystal fountain out of silence sings
A voice all warmth and dazzle like the sun on snow,
As music calls out from its source the living rivers,
Touches the heart at quick, at its unguarded deep,
Where sit the naked joys, where leaps and shivers
The locked light in the breast, and wakes from sleep—
As music in a silence so sometimes passion stands
Imperious as an angel, touches the secret sources,
Moves from the eyes down to the sleeping hands,
A fiery liquor, through each passage courses,
Sets fountains in the flesh and in the sounding heart
A deeper crying as if floating sphere and sphere,
Swung out in space forever, terribly apart,
Sang to each other softly across wastes of air—
So fiery-soft, so swift the angel passion brings,
As music in a still house out of silence springs.

3

Passion like radium is luminous in essence,
Sleeps in the day, suffers not, neither knows its joy,
Until the dark reveals its incandescence,
Potent and startling as a naked boy,—
It shines, stripped of all softness, a fierce light,
Burns love like metal till the white-hot fuel
Flowers in fireworks through the body's night,
And in that instant, marvelous and cruel,
He who has born this wonder in his breast
Like radium is luminous, is pure, is blest.

4

The wind which swept the earth has mounted the trees.
We sit in a quiet below the leaf-blown skies,
Silence touches our eyelids and enfolds our knees,
Breaks blue as butterfly-wings across your eyes.

The wind which crackled the leaves along the path
Has risen up, has flown to the tops of the trees.
Here there is silence and a quiet aftermath:
Passion that shook our eyelids and our knees

Now takes its way to the heart in a quiet flood.
Silence touches our eyelids. We find sleep good.

If there is mercy it is not, no, not in the wind,
In the trees restless, in the blood wild and bitter,
Tearing apart the roses no gentle sun can mend,
Bending the yielding branch, banging the shutter—
If there is mercy for the heart, the crying savage
It is not in the wind that turns the blood to air,
Sweeps through the garden it has come to ravage,
Opens the secret rose and lays its center bare,—
If there is mercy it is somewhere absolutely still
Where the light-tortured head may come to rest,—
If there is mercy beyond the wind's wild will
Where are the silences this love has blessed?
Where have they gone, that we are seized by the wild,
That we are so invaded and so shaken,
O love, what have you done to your heart's child,
That she goes hunted and by peace forsaken,
If there is mercy for the heart, if there is peace to keep,
Where is it but sealed up, or unremembered, in your
    hand asleep?

6

Alone one is never lonely: the spirit adventures, waking
In a quiet garden, in a cool house, abiding single there;
The spirit adventures in sleep, the sweet thirst-slaking
When only the moon's reflection touches the wild hair.
There is no place more intimate than the spirit alone:
It finds a lovely certainty in the evening and the morning.
It is only where two have come together bone against bone
That those alonenesses take place, when, without warning
The sky opens over their heads to an infinite hole in space;
It is only turning at night to a lover that one learns
He is set apart like a star forever and that sleeping face
(For whom the heart has cried, for whom the frail hand
    burns)
Is swung out in the night alone, so luminous and still,
The waking spirit attends, the loving spirit gazes
Without communion, without touch, and comes to know
    at last
Out of a silence only and never when the body blazes
That love is present, that always burns alone, however
    steadfast.

7

To stand on the earth again is a grave event
After a journey on a sea so deeply moving,
After the fluid, cruelly shining moment
To plant foot on the earth strange to our loving,
We who are foreigners come from the heart's silence,
Who move in a present flowing from the past,
Who go garlanded in a peace, private, intense,
Who go bearing a silent city in the breast—
That city where a cloud-like swan is amorous
Of a cool fountain repeating kisses like a fluid tree,
Embracing snow with tears crystal and clamorous:
For your remembered images take part of me.
There is no past that does not move within this measure,
No child you were, or I, not understood,
No love that does not add its weight to this new treasure,
To these two lovers standing in a little wood.

8

That night we went outside the gate beyond the wood
Where nothing is but the ploughed earth and open sky.
We went together as the sun set. There we stood
Holding the heavens in the tiny iris of the eye,
The whole earth sitting in that fragile orb:
The light poured down unearthly on a further field,
A radiance the spirit all drank in, all did absorb.
And then the portent vanished as it came, to yield
Earth to the homely dark while, human-hearted,
We turned to find our way, the heaven in our eyes
Turned toward home, and from those miracles
    departed,—
Thinking it were not good, it were not wholly wise
Now to endure the dark, but wise to come to places
Where we should find that light upon our faces.

9

There are voices in the garden. Day folds itself into
     twilight.
The windows are wide open to the evening wind on the
     leaf.
From the dark everything outside looks delicate and
     bright,
The heavy roses slumber in the garden where there is no
     grief:
I am a silence only under the imperious human cries,
I cannot move out of my darkness to the places where
     they glow.
I cannot reach the careless voices of the living where
     they rise
(They sound like cold flutes in the twilight and they do
     not know
Their poignance, how it moves through the heart like
     an icy breath):
O bright voice of love, what have you done, what have
     you done to speak to me of death?

The spirit comes back to silence like a dove,
Wings shut, poising herself upon the quiet bough;
Her brilliant eyes are open but they do not move,
Who sits, wild and aloof, and like a dove does coo,
Does make unto herself this curious moan,
Does lay her voice upon the air as if to plead
The very loving wind to leave her there alone,
To give a quiet to the quick beat in the blood,
To let her poise on silence till that silence perish,
To let her shelter in the shadowed leaf,
Till the wild wind return, her heart-beats cherish,
The passion that has wrung her breast like grief.

II

We sat smoking at a table by the river
And then suddenly in the silence someone said,
'Look at the sunlight on the apple-tree there shiver:
I shall remember that long after I am dead.'
Together we all turned to see how the tree shook,
How it sparkled and seemed spun out of green and
    gold,
And we thought that hour, that light and our long
    mutual look
Might warm us each someday when we were cold.

And I thought of your face that sweeps over me like
    light,
Like the sun on the apple making a lovely show,
So one seeing it marvelled the other night,
Turned to me saying, 'What is it in your heart? You
    glow.'
Not guessing that on my face he saw the singular
Reflection of your grace like fire on snow—
And loved you there.

12

Now it is evening coming and you are not here
But listen to the sound in this small horn,
But shield with its cool whorl your secret ear,
Listen as in a shell to 'fairy seas forlorn',
Until near things are far, far things are near.

The chinese pinks make magic on the summer air,
Do you feel it? There is a blackbird singing
In the hedge beside you. Do you almost hear?
And very far away the low bell ringing,
My love, now it is evening, are you there?

Will you not come? For evening is a spell:
Far things draw near, near things vanish away,
And love is the secret, love the delicate shell
To waft you over the deep, the watery way—
Here are the pinks, the blackbird, the low bell.

Is it a flower pressed or a perfect leaf
To be laid away, to be discovered again—
The pattern of a joy, the shadow of a grief,
The precise contour of a previous pain?

Wilder than these are, dearer and deeper,
Remembrance is a bird free in the mind,
That sings sometimes to the dream-captured sleeper
Like light upon the eyelids of the blind.

Not to be fondled like a coloured toy,
This bird wilder than any, swifter of wing
Illuminates the dark hour with its joy—
But only when it chooses will it sing.

Pursue it through the labyrinthine wood,
A nightingale is not more secret of a sigh—
Then out of nowhere ices the warm blood
And stops the heart with its sweet wringing cry!

WINTER LANDSCAPE

FROM MEN WHO DIED DELUDED

★

This is the time to speak to those who will come after,
To those who will climb the mountain-tops although
The continual clouds have crept down upon us
And we cannot tell any more how far there is to go.

This is the time to set our lips upon great horns and blow
Far down the years a note to reach them when
They are failing on the crest before the end,
To fall on their ears like a sweet hail from men

Who did not reach so far but blessed their march,
From men who died deluded, far below the peak,
The self-destroyed, unwilling, blinded, caught,
Yet who believed, yet who desired to speak—

Dying, to blow a horn for those who would come after,
Despairing, to send up one clear note from the edge of
    death
And as the victors falter to salute them proudly
With the hope we cherished with our final breath.

This is the time, this dark time, this bewildered
To give our mortal lives that the great peaceful places
May surely be attained by those who, when they falter,
Must be confronted by the living vision on our dead faces.

AFTERNOON ON WASHINGTON STREET

*

Walking on this dark day through the bewildering city
I came to a familiar street where always shabby men
Stand watching with dull eyes too tired for pity
The news' despatches written up in chalk for them,
And that indifferent watching held me in suspense,
Fastened my eyes to the same writing they had stopped
    to read:
Here was the world, bitter and full of wrong and
    without sense;
Here were the men who soon would be chalked up
    among the shabby dead.
And then I glanced down to a sign among the others
    written
Of one who on this very day, and in defence of Milton,
    spoke
Against the curse of Eliot and Pound and I was smitten
With fire at the heart's cockle to think of poet's work.
Cromwell, I could have cried out to the startled and the
    dour,
Cromwell is dead. There is no one to care a penny for
    those wars
But Milton lives, Milton is living at this desperate
    hour—
Milton, keeping the dark night of the spirit full of stars!

THE PURITAN

*

Once he was seduced by the soft luxurious hill,
The peace-inducing landscape, interminably green,
Where rivers are shallow, full of flowers and still,
Where the rain is gentle, falling without spleen.

Today he thinks of the bare pastures and the cedar trees,
The bitter land where a child is hardy and learns
To be fearful of his heart, to be wary of what he feels
Hiding among the juniper bushes and the brown ferns.

He remembers the stone walls marking field from field,
Piled up out of infinite stones by the patient hand,
He thinks of the thin harvest that those pastures yield,
How the men are lean men, how it is a stern land.

He thinks of a country where roots are durable and deep,
Where the speech has a tang in it and is never mild,
Where the kind of peace is the snow coming sometimes
    like sleep,
So cold it would freeze up the tears of a soft child.

FROM A TRAIN-WINDOW

★

There is nothing terrible in this landscape,
The sea frozen in the marshes and a yellow sun
Going down gleaming over the ice, foretelling snow—
There is nothing in it at all like terror or escape,
Yet in this spacious stillness death has won;
Sooner or later summer has had to go.
There is nothing really to fear in a world grown old,
Nothing like terror in what lies so white,
Yet this is the very outline of defeat and cold,
The picture of a world bitten with blight.
Even the children, gallant, fragile-skinned,
Brush the tears from their eyes, whipped by the wind.

STATIC LANDSCAPE

★

Orchards sleep. Rivers are arrested in their flow;
Under a brilliant heaven the ploughed fields glitter,
Jacketed in ice, bright with the sterile snow.
This landscape, curiously static, brilliant, bitter
Proclaims the long blank in the winter season,
Tells how much waiting the stubborn buried root
Endures where it is locked, suggests the reason
For silence before the struggle in the springing shoot.

CONSIDERATIONS

★

I am not native to this country so it captures my mind
With no conflict of ownership, no bitterness of blood,
No root in the body straining to find its food, but blind:
I stand on this hill, a stranger; I walk in this wood
Eyes open for the single pleasure of seeing,
Ears pleased as they listen to the seeping and the crush
Of snow on the boughs, and here I am simply being.
I am standing apart in the wood, attentive to its hush:
It is not in possession that the mind achieves its peace
Nor does its better work. Perhaps the perfect will
Is in negation first when thinking seems to cease,
When mind surveys a landscape absolutely still,
And passionless observes the snow and the bough's
        strain
As if not native to the earth,—aloof and foreign.

WINTER EVENING

*

The evenings are spun glass these winter days;
They stretch out clear above the dusty litter,
They quietly surround with a pale crystal haze,—
But just before the dark these evenings glitter.
Then for one moment under that clear glass
The fragile earth, the trees, all seem to shiver,
While hangs there, still, most beautiful and ominous,
The darkening sky reflected in the river,
While people peer out just before they pull
The comfortable shades and shut themselves away
From all that's ominous and beautiful,
From what they guess the night might have to say.

MAP FOR DESPAIR

*

It is true that you live on a cold continent,
A mental climate of your own.
More than the shape of a cloud
You cannot expect,
The occasional magic of a storm of snow—
You can ask no more of it.
This is your island, created by yourself,
Set in a space without horizon:
A ship might offer an escape,
A waving human arm might tempt with hope,
Might pull the little stone out of your breast
And substitute the magic and disaster of a face.
Now you have won this island,
Protect it with your utmost strength.
Pillow your head on your arm.
And for your loneliness at night,
And for your terrors,
There is the certain morning,
And for that question with no answer,
The careless comfort of the elements.

YOU WHO ASK PEACE

★

You who ask peace, peace is not in your nature,
    You cannot hope to rest,
Born as you were with that implacable creature
    Rooted in your breast.

Adamant is the heart, adamant, lonely, cruel,
    Beating against the bone,
Asking a savage question, the necessary fuel
    By which it lives alone.

Asking a savage question and not resigned,
    The starving heart
Takes its revenge upon the nobler mind
    And tears your peace apart.

THE PRIDE OF TREES

★

On a dark night I thought of the pride of trees.
Have you seen them, unresistant, wholly granted
To the temper of the wind as if a curious ease
Came to the branches from the root, deep-planted.

Have you seen them in summer, fountains pouring
Green plumes on the twilight, magical,
Movement arrested at the point of soaring,
Waters held frozen in grace as they fall.

Have you seen them winter in the bleak air,
The stiff unburied leaves blown at their side,
The delicate and constant structure standing bare?—
On a dark night I thought of the trees' pride.

Wondering if one could learn to bend like these,
Achieve in violence and grief this kind of pride,
Grant oneself wholly to the difficult mysteries,
Yet still in structure steadfast and in peace abide.

GREETING

New Year's Eve, 1937

*

The earth feels old tonight
And we who live and stand on the cold rim
Face a new year.
It is raining everywhere
As if the rain were mercy,
As if the rain were peace,
Peace falling on our hair.
Open your hearts tonight; let them burn!
Let them light a way in the dark.
Let them one by one affirm
There is hope for a staff:
I say it will flower in our hands,
We shall go garlanded.
There is the fine fresh stuff of faith for a coat:
We shall go warm.
We shall go on by the light of our hearts.
We shall burn mightily in the new year.
We shall go on together—
O you who stand alone on the rim of the earth and are
     cold,
I salute you here!

A Letter to James Stephens

James, it is snowing here. It is November.
Think of the good day when we talked together,
For it is time to think of it, remember
What the warm wine, warm friendship, summer weather
Raised in our minds now that it is so cold,
Now that we sit alone and half the world apart,
This bitter season when the young grow old
And sit indoors to weigh the fiery heart:
What of it now? What of this personal all,
The little world these hands have tried to fashion
Using a single theme for their material,
Always a human heart, a human passion?
You said 'Seek for a sterner stuff than this,
Look out of your closed spaces to the infinite,
Look beyond hunger and the longed-for kiss
To what there is beyond your love and in it,
To the whole heavy earth and all it bears;
Support the sky. Know the path of the planet,
Until you stand alone, a man who stares
His loneliness out of its depth to span it,
Till you can chisel substance out of space.
Forget your love, your little war, your ache;
Forget that haunting so mysterious face
And write for an abstracted beauty's sake.
Contain a large world in a small strict plan,
Your job is to draw out the essence and provide

The word that will endure, comfort, sustain a man.
This is your honour. This should be your pride.'
Dear James, pure poet, I see you with that shell
Held to your sensitive abstracted ear,
Hunting the ocean's rumour till you hear it well,
Until you can set down the sound you hear:—
Fixed to a shell like that you made immortal,
This heart listens, this fragile auricle
Holds rumour like your ocean's, is a portal
That sometimes opens to contain the miracle.
If there are miracles we can record
They happen in the places that you curse.
Blessèd the pure in heart and the enduring word
Sings of that love that spins the universe.
My honour (and I cherish it for it is hardly won)
Is to be pure in this: is to believe
That to write down these perishable songs for one,
For one alone, and out of love, is not to grieve
But to build on the quicksand of despair
A house where every man may take his ease,
May come to shelter from the outer air,
A little house where he may find his peace.
Dear James, if this fire seems only the strange
Quick-burning fire of youth unfounded on the earth
Then may it be transformed but never change.
Let Him in whose great hands lie death and birth
Preserve its essence like that bush of flame
That stood up in a path, and, fiery-plumed,
Contained the angel who could speak God's name—
The bush that burned and still was not consumed.

64

Et ne me réponds pas si le printemps est mort—

JEAN DOMINIQUE

ENCOUNTER IN APRIL
(1929–1933)

FIRST SNOW

*

This is the first soft snow
That tiptoes up to your door
As you sit by the fire and sew,
That sifts through a crack in the floor
And covers your hair with hoar.

This is the stiffening wound
Burning the heart of a deer
Chased by a moon-white hound,
This is the hunt and the queer
Sick beating of feet that fear.

This is the crisp despair
Lying close to the marrow,
Fallen out of the air
Like frost on the narrow
Bone of a shot sparrow.

This is the love that will seize
Savagely onto your mind
And do whatever he please,
This the despair, and a moon-blind
Hound you will never bind.

CONCEPTION

She shall be called woman—Genesis ii, 23

I

She did not cry out
nor move.
She lay quite still
and leaned
against the great curve
of the earth,
and her breast
was like a fruit
bursten of its own sweetness.

She did not move
nor cry out—
she only looked down
at the hand
against her breast.
She looked down
at the naked hand
and wept.

She could not yet endure
this delicate savage
to lie upon her.
She could not yet endure
the blood to beat so there.
She could not cope
with the first ache
of fullness.

She lay quite still
and looked down
at the hand
where blood was locked
and longed to loose the blood
and let it flow
over her breast
like rain.

She did not move
nor cry out.
She lay beneath the hand
conceiving of a flower,
the flower of love—
she bore it like a child.

2

Not on the earth
but surely somewhere
between the elements
of air and sea
she lay that night,
no rim of bone to mark
where body clove to body
and no separate flesh,
strangely impenetrable—
O somewhere surely
did she come
to that clear turquoise place
where sky and water meet

and lay transparent there,
knowing the wave.

3

She bore the wound of desire
and it did not close,
though she had tried
to burn her hand
and turn one pain
into a simpler pain—
yet it did not close.

She had not known
how strong
the body's will,
how intricate
the stirring of its litheness
that lay now
unstrung,
like a bow—
she saw herself
disrupted at the center
and torn.

And she went into the sea
because her core ached
and there was no healing.

4

Not in denial, her peace.
For there in the sea

where she had wished
to leave her body
like a little garment,
she saw now
that not by severing this
would finity be ended
and the atom die,
not so the pure abstract
exist alone.
From those vast places
she must come back
into her particle.
She must put on again
the little garment
of hunger.
Not in denial
her appeasement,
not yet.

5

For a long time
it would be pain
and weakness,
and she who worshipped
all straight things
and the narrow breast
would lie relaxed
like an animal asleep,
without strength.

For a long time
a consciousness possessed her
that felt into all grief
as if it were a wound
within herself—
a mouse with its tiny shriek
would leave her
drained and spent.

The unanswerable body
seemed
held in an icy pity
for all livingness—
that was itself
initiate.

6

And then one day
all feeling
slipped out from her skin,
until no finger's consciousness remained,
no pain—
and she all turned
to earth
like abstract gravity.
She did not know
how she had come
to close her separate lids
nor where she learned
the gesture of her sleeping,

yet something in her slept
most deeply,
and something in her
lay like stone
under a folded dress—
she could not tell how long.

7

Her body was a city
where the soul
had lain asleep,
and now she woke.
She was aware
down to extremity
of how herself was charged,
fibre electric,—
a hand under her breast
could hear the dynamo.
A hand upon her wrist
could feel the pulse beat,
imminent.
She felt the atoms stir,
the myriad expand
and stir.

She looked at her hand—
the mesh
with its multitude of lines,
the exquisite small hairs,
the veins

finding their way
down to the nails,
the nails themselves
set in so firmly
with half-moons
at their base,
the fine-set bone,
knuckle and sinew,
and she examined
the mysterious legend
upon the palm—
this was her hand,
a present someone had given her.

And she looked at her breasts
that were firm and full,
standing straightly
out from her chest,
and were each a city
mysteriously part
of other cities.
The earth itself
was not more intricate,
more lovely
than these two
cupped in her hands,
heavy in her hands.
Nothing ever was
as wonderful as this.

8

She let her hands
go softly down her skin,
the curving rib,
soft belly
and slim thigh.
She let her hands slip down
as if they held a shift
and she were trying it
for the first time,
a shining supple garment
she would not want to lose:
So did she clothe herself.

9

She would not ever be naked
again—
She would not know
that nakedness
that stretches to the brim
and finds no shelter
from the pure terrific
light of space.
The finite self
had gathered
and was born
out of the infinite,
was hers,
and whole.

75

For the first time
she knew what it meant
to be made so
and moulded into this shape
of a pear,
this heaviness of curving fruit.

10

There were seeds
within her
that burst at intervals
and for a little while
she would come back
to heaviness,
and then before a surging miracle of blood
relax,
and re-identify herself,
each time more closely
with the heart of life:
'I am the beginning,
the never-ending,
the perfect tree.'
And she would lean
again as once
on the great curve of the earth,
part of its turning,
as distinctly part
of the universe as a star—
as unresistant,
as complete.

SUMMER LANDSCAPE

FROM CORNWALL

*

It was then that I looked down from the steep cliff
And saw a village with the sea beating against it,
Gray houses huddled, a wall, a yellow skiff,
And there stood a boy and girl, their heads bent,—
Wrapped in a loneliness, they did not move.
They stood there with a hand's breadth between them
And in that silent space was all their love.
Never-to-be-forgotten, mind-engraved that scene—
They looked like figures in an allegory,
And as they stood quite still and face to face
All partings and all meetings lay before me,
The heart of man split open and the pure jet
Of anguish or of joy that springs from the cleft.
I turned home then like a man who has seen
A fountain spurt out of the rock and is bereft
Of speech, yet wanting to tell every man he meets.

THE TREES

★

Now trees take on their wonder,
beech and laburnum, saffron fountains,
the candled chestnut, ballerina elms,
the hawthorn curving pink umbrellas over lovers—
This is England. This is summer.
The trees sparkle. They look each morning new.
They are hardly rooted at all—
Their leaves might lift them tomorrow
to another planet on a thousand wings.
They are tourists here. They rustle.
The trees are all young today,
all ascension, lifting up of flowers:
How beautiful their coming.
How beautiful their visitation on us,
green as green taffeta, publishing hope,
making the silken sound of summer!

WEEK END

★

The taste of figs and cream, cool slipping down your
     throat,
the crisp white dresses gleaming against green,
the ping of tennis balls on the clipped grassy coat,
the brilliant voices, sudden silences, the wells
birds fill with liquid flutes and watery sounds,
the summer rustle purring in the leaves.
Lie here and let sun suck the marrow of distress,
change it to a fantastic dream, a nursery rhyme, a game
(You used to play it) 'Still Pond, no more moving.'
The old kind-hearted dog will come to be caressed,
the cat with barley-sugar eyes run after bees
and then come back to rub against your knees.
Lie here face down and slip off into sleep;
Lie here at last and soak the sum of gentleness
into your veins.
This is the England dreamed of, the island of content,
the changeless statue in a garden,
the still pond, moving not.

ON HAMPSHIRE DOWNS

★

Will any English heart leap as mine who am foreign
    here,
The full sweep of the downs break over his mind like
    this,
When he thinks of the rabbits running to warren there,
And thatching and shearing in Hampshire villages—
The saffron mustard-fields and blue-green corn in
    pattern
With the pewits starting up and giving their sharp call,
The larks never out of breath, and a cuckoo, far-off
    slattern
Asking a lazy question that has no answer at all—
The hedges laced over with may and its scent on the air,
The brooks full of soft gray trout, immobile,
    listening—
The brooks all yellow with buttercups and daisies there,
A paradise for plucking out of plump fish glistening:
Will any English heart leap as mine when I think of
    the hill
Where I stood and looked at the sweep of the downs to
    the South
Where England lay at my feet so wonderfully still,
Where I stood for a long time with my heart in my
    mouth?

NURSERY RHYME

FOR POLLY WHOSE EYES ARE TIRED

★

Shut your eyes then
And let us slip
Out of the city rain
Into a special ship,
Call her *The Pilgrim*
Set sail and go
Over the world's rim
To where Rousseau
Discovered a jungle
Of indigo trees,
A marvelous tangle:
Precise oranges,
Tigers with dreaming eyes,
Larger and larger flowers,
Leaves of gigantic size—
Wander for hours
Under a crimson sun
In a pale milky sky
With a vermilion
Lizard near by,
And over it all
The strangeness that hovers
Like a green pall,
Envelopes and covers

In a warm still suspense
All of the landscape
Like a sixth sense—
Till there is no escape,
Till in the grasses
(Two people Rousseau
Saw through his glasses
And wanted to know)
You who have shut your eyes
And I who brought you here
Are to our great surprise
Part of the atmosphere,
Part of the painter's dream,
Of his most intent seeing
In a place where things seem
Instead of being,
No longer living, no longer mortal,
Fabulous ladies,
Unreal, immortal—
Shut then your open eyes
Let us go softly home,
Back to the sleeping ship
Over the emerald foam,
Over the edge and slip
Out of the Rousseau world
Into the world of men,
Sails all bound up and furled:
Open your eyes again!

BERCEUSE

★

The evenings are as white as milk, my child.
The sea is very silent.
There are no birds.
There is no other way than peace.
Your large eyes
open like two lanterns
seem curiously blind—
Your two hands folded
on a smooth stone from the beach
are cool and senseless
as the halves of some quite icy fruit.
It is the country
of the milk-white evenings
where you shall go, my child,
living and dying,
to sleep, to sleep.

SONNETS:
ENCOUNTER IN APRIL

SONNETS: ENCOUNTER IN APRIL

I

We came together softly like two deer,
Their horns in velvet still, erect and slight,
Their fur like silk, their large eyes amber-clear,
Startled and dazzled in each other's light.
We stood quite still together face to face,
Untrembling, unaware, remote from love,
Beguiled there simply by each other's grace,
Not moving—O we did not want to move.
We stood quite still like two deer in a wood,
Knowing a silence exquisite and wild,
Chilled into crystal the mercurial blood,
The heart fierce and transparent as a child:
We came together softly in great wonder,
Not dreaming of this lightning-love, this thunder!

2

Love, fall as softly on his lids as sleep,
Come softly to his heart lest he should tell
The thief who steals into his citadel
To ravish treasure from the inmost keep:
Love, come upon him warily and deep.
For if he startle first it were as well
To bind a fox's throat with a gold bell
As hold him when it is his will to leap.
Let him believe it is himself who chooses
To leave that crag for a most human bed,
O let him think it is his will that loses
Feet of an antelope to lay his head
Against my knee—and may he never know
That it was love itself that willed it so.

We who had been so wounded and so cloven
Were grafted like two trees into one bark
And our two colors sharply interwoven,
The delicate and bright, the tawny dark;
Out of our mingled blood, petal and flower
With a strange fertile perfume of its own,
Love came upon us softly in that hour—
We did not see that love lay there alone.
And when we woke out of the dream she made
Nothing had changed—the earth was just the
    same,
And we, so wounded, strangers and afraid,
Standing apart saying each other's name,
Looked down, and saw love, luminous and wild,
Lying between us like a sleeping child.

4

Here in this narrow bed infinity is ours.
We who are lovers can corrupt the night,
Set the stars spinning and the planet-towers,
The great triumphant cities in their flight:
We are the masters of those desolate spaces.
We find the place where time has never been,
Where the bright vision falls across our faces,
Silence that is imperious and serene.
We are the night and all the stars are streaming
Like mercury down to the luminous heart.
You hold me in your arms. We are not dreaming—
Until the cruel light tears us apart,
Light that must find us pitiful and human,
Upon the narrow bed, the mortal woman.

5

If I have poured myself without reserve,
Telling you all and holding nothing back
To be resource against the lightning-swerve
That, soon or late, a changing heart must take—
If I have seemed too prodigal of light,
Winding it round you like a bright blue cloak
Over your eyes to hood you from the night—
If you have wondered sometimes when I spoke,
Drawing up words like water for your cup,
Out of what well they came, how deep, how clear,
How long before a drought would dry it up—
I did it for the sake of love, my dear:
It will be well to know, if the glass splinter,
There have been honest words before the winter.

6

For you a leopard-word—no deer, no pheasant,
No gentle creature shall the mind devise—
For you a leopard, lithe and arrogant,
Wild as wild honey with clear golden eyes,
A word, born in the tropic of the mind,
A savage lissome word that men have found,
Men who were beautiful and strong and kind
Although less subtly, difficultly bound
Than I who find it now, and call it mine,
And leash it firmly with a binding-thong—
The leopard whose clear eyes are gold as wine,
The word, elusive, hunted in a song—
I give it to you now. Take off your glove
And tame it with bare hands: the word is love!

7

Somewhere there is delight love will not bring
And peace more deep than any love could borrow;
Death is a slight thing and a lovely thing
And when the heart dies it knows not of sorrow.
Somewhere there is a peace for each peace broken
And we may turn away and lie apart
In sudden loneliness with no word spoken,
The still frost falls so lightly on the heart.
And we may lie down in the dark asunder
And learn a separate peace love did not know;
Frost on the heart can turn to a sharp wonder
And the hot hand that ached lie cool as snow:
So shall we wake who have slept unaware
That as we slept, death lay upon our hair.

8

There comes a moment when the gentle flesh
Denies itself as if it apprehended
Woven across its own, sublimer mesh
Of earthly and angelic substance blended.
That dearest element of earth abstains
From tasting the fulfilment of delight,
Translates the fire to crystal in its veins
As if a fervent blood could burn too bright
And grow beyond the regions of the soul,
Destroying in a fury of sensation
Love that was built upon the mind's control:
There comes a moment of almost cessation
When pulse itself is bound and dares not move
So deep is loneliness, so deep is love.

9

Now let me rest. Now let me lay my hand
Upon yours, as cool, as smooth as stone.
Keep it. Hold it as holds the clear-ribbed sand
A wave's shape after the wave has gone.
Let no wind come to blow the lashes down
Between our eyes that look each into each
As a faun looks at that sea-changed faun
Reflected in a pool. Let the bronze beach
Color our mind alone with sand and space.
All that we gave, or lost, or took in pain
Forgotten as wind is in this windless place,
Forgotten as noise of wind driving the rain.
Now let us rest. Now let us lay my hand
In yours—like a smooth stone on the smooth sand.

STRANGERS

★

There have been two strangers
 Who met within a wood
And looked once at each other
 Where they stood.

And there have been two strangers
 Who met among the heather
And did not look at all
 But lay down together.

And there have been two strangers
 Who met an April day
And looked long at each other,—
 And went their way.

Made in the USA
Coppell, TX
16 October 2021